2/07

03-09 ③

6 C10
2/11

# STEGOSAURUS

## REVISED EDITION

A TRUE BOOK®

by

**Elaine Landau**

**Children's Press®**
A Division of Scholastic Inc.

New York  Toronto  London  Auckland  Sydney
Mexico City  New Delhi  Hong Kong
Danbury, Connecticut

**Stegosaurus** is known for the several plates that ran along its back.

Content Consultant
**Susan H. Gray, MS, Zoology,**
*Little Rock, Arkansas*

*Reading Consultant*
**Cecilia Minden-Cupp, PhD**
*Former Director, Language and
Literacy Program
Harvard Graduate School of
Education*

*Author's Dedication*
**For Emily**

*The photograph on the cover
and on the title page shows a
model of* Stegosaurus.

Library of Congress Cataloging-in-Publication Data
Landau, Elaine.
    Stegosaurus  / by Elaine Landau. — Rev. ed.
        p. cm. — (A true book)
    Includes index.
    ISBN-10: 0-531-16830-1 (lib. bdg.)        0-531-15474-2 (pbk.)
    ISBN-13: 978-0-531-16830-1 (lib. bdg.)     978-0-531-15474-8 (pbk.)
    1. Stegosaurus —Juvenile literature. I. Title. II. Series.
QE862.O65L35 2007
567.915'3–dc22

                                                            2005037537

CHILDREN'S PRESS, and A TRUE BOOK™, and associated logos are
trademarks and/or registered trademarks of Scholastic Library Publishing.
SCHOLASTIC and associated logos are trademarks and/or registered
trademarks of Scholastic Inc.
    2 3 4 5 6 7 8 9 10 R 16 15 14 13 12 11 10 09 08 07          08

# Contents

*Stegosaurus* lived in what is now North America.

# At the Start

Can you imagine the world 150 million years ago? There were no people. Instead, large, leathery-skinned **reptiles** called dinosaurs roamed Earth. It was the Age of the Dinosaurs. During that time, a lot of different dinosaurs existed. Among these was *Stegosaurus.*

Like all dinosaurs, *Stegosaurus* was a **prehistoric** reptile. It lived in North America. If you had been alive back then, you might have seen this large dinosaur roaming through what are now Colorado, Utah, and Wyoming. These states were *Stegosaurus* land millions of years ago.

*Stegosaurus* might have wandered down a bicycle path you now use. Or maybe it

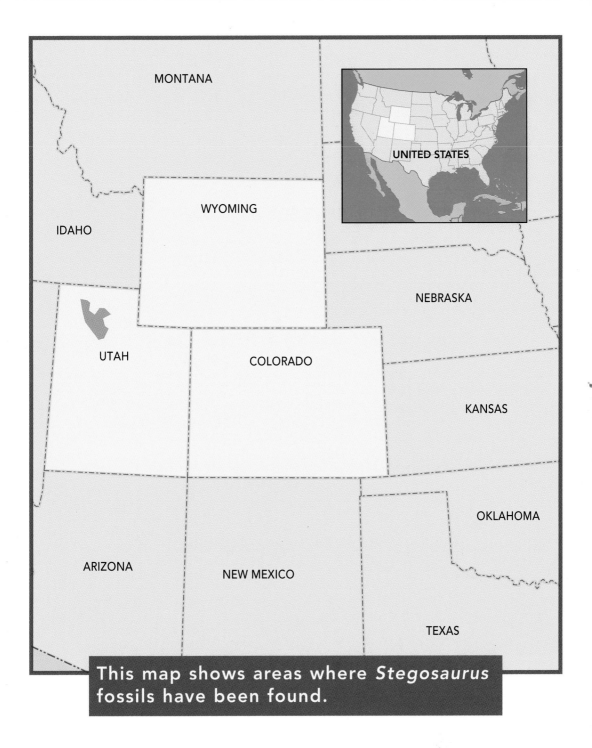

This map shows areas where *Stegosaurus* fossils have been found.

looked for food in your backyard. Imagine looking out your window and seeing a 12,000-pound (5,443-kilogram), 30-foot (9-meter)-long dinosaur instead of your dog!

That was *Stegosaurus*. If you want to know more about how this dinosaur looked and lived, read on.

# A Close-up Look

*Stegosaurus* was an unusual-looking animal. This dinosaur had a large, bulky body supported by four strong legs. Its hind, or back, legs were twice as long as its front legs. The long hind legs caused the dinosaur's body

to slope forward from its hips to its head.

Stegosaurus's front feet have been compared to an elephant's. Each foot had a sturdy padded base and five short, wide toes. *Stegosaurus* also had a blunt claw on each front toe. Each hind foot had three toes with blunt claws.

*Stegosaurus's* small head looked unusual on such a huge animal. Its head was only about 16 inches (41 centimeters) long. That was just a fraction of the size of the dinosaur's other body parts. *Stegosaurus's* brain was also tiny. It was about the size of a walnut.

Paleontologists—scientists who study prehistoric life— wondered about *Stegosaurus's* brain. They could not under- stand how such a massive

*Stegosaurus* had a small head for such a large dinosaur.

dinosaur could have had such a small brain. Some paleontologists thought that *Stegosaurus* had a second brain in the back of its spine. This second brain would have controlled the dinosaur's back feet and tail. This was shown not to be true.

Perhaps *Stegosaurus*'s strangest feature was the double row of seventeen thin, bony plates. These plates jutted out from the dinosaur's neck, back, and tail. The plates were staggered along the dinosaur's back and looked like arrowheads. No two plates were the same size. The largest plates were about 3 feet (1 m) high, or about the length of a hockey stick.

A close-up view of *Stegosaurus's* bony plates

The word *Stegosaurus* means "roofed lizard." The name suits this dinosaur well because the plates along its back overlapped like the shingles of a roof.

Some paleontologists think that the plates might have helped the dinosaur control its body temperature. The plates may have collected heat when *Stegosaurus* needed to warm up.

*Stegosaurus* is known as one of the **armored** dinosaurs. Its throat was also covered with many small, bony disks. These served as extra protection for the dinosaur. Some of *Stegosaurus*'s relatives had disk-shaped plates over their hips as well. At the end of *Stegosaurus*'s tail were pairs of large, sharply pointed spikes. Each of these was 2 to 3 feet (.6 to 1 m) long.

*Stegosaurus*'s bony plates might have helped the dinosaur warm up or cool down when needed.

# A Dumb Dino?

*Stegosaurus*'s brain was small because it had such a small head.

There is no sure way to measure how smart a dinosaur was. Scientists have found, though, that an animal whose brain is larger than expected for its body size is usually smart. Human beings are thought to be very smart since our brains are quite large for our bodies.

Stegosaurus's brain was very small compared to its body size. So paleontologists think it probably was not very smart. Perhaps in *Stegosaurus*'s world it was more important to have a strong body with a lot of armored plates than a large brain.

Paleontologists do not know what color *Stegosaurus* was. They think that armored dinosaurs may have been brightly colored. *Stegosaurus*'s bright red, green, or yellow skin could have been useful as a warning to **predators**. Bright colors could have also been helpful in attracting a mate.

# Dinosaur Dining

*Stegosaurus* was an herbivore, or plant eater. It roamed through forests looking for plants to eat. Most paleontologists think that *Stegosaurus* used its low-hanging head to spot and eat plants that grew close to the ground. Its larger hind legs might have sometimes allowed the dinosaur to stand up on its back legs to reach higher bushes and trees.

*Stegosaurus* grazed on low-growing plants and grasses.

# All in the Family

*S*tegosaurus was in a family of dinosaurs known as stegosaurids. Stegosaurids ranged in length from about 10 to 30 feet (3 to 9 m) long. All of these dinosaurs were plant eaters. All had some kind of bony plating on their bodies.

*Kentrosaurus* was a stegosaurid that lived in present-day Africa.

*Stegosaurus* was among the largest dinosaurs in this family. It was also the only stegosaurid in North America. Other stegosaurids could be found in Africa, India, Europe, and China.

Many dinosaurs lived in groups, or herds. However, scientists think that *Stegosaurus*, as well as other dinosaurs in its family, were loners. Their skeletons are usually found far from others of their own kind.

23

Jutting out from the tip of *Stegosaurus*'s snout was a horn-covered beak. *Stegosaurus* may have used its beak to rip twigs and branches off shrubs. It might have also used its beak to pull plants out of the ground.

*Stegosaurus* had leaf-shaped teeth set in rows at the back of its mouth. Its teeth were not strong enough to grind up food. So the dinosaur probably swallowed

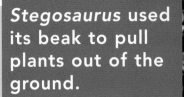

*Stegosaurus* used its beak to pull plants out of the ground.

its food whole. These meals may have remained in its stomach for several days.

# Defenses in a Prehistoric World

*Stegosaurus* had to defend itself against meat-eating predators. Some of these predators were larger than *Stegosaurus*. *Stegosaurus* may have also been **prey** for groups of smaller meat eaters that attacked in packs, such as *Velociraptor*.

*Stegosaurus* had some defenses. *Stegosaurus* could lash its enemy with its spiked, muscular tail. The hard, sharp spikes could rip open a predator's flesh.

*Stegosaurus*'s bony plates may have also protected the dinosaur against attacks. If a predator was nearby, *Stegosaurus* may have turned sideways and showed its

*Stegosaurus* defends itself against an attack by *Tyrannosaurus rex.*

plates to make itself appear bigger. You may have seen an angry cat do the same thing when it arches its back and its fur stands up.

Paleontologists have also found that a large amount of blood could flow through *Stegosaurus*'s plates. This blood flow might have caused the plates to "blush," or darken in color. This would have made them stand out against the green and brown of the plant life nearby. The effect would have made *Stegosaurus* appear even more threatening.

Putting together dinosaur skeletons like these has taught paleontologists a lot about prehistoric animals.

# Hooked on Dinosaurs

Paleontologists learn about dinosaurs from **fossils**. Fossils are evidence of plants and animals that lived long ago. Fossils might include bones, footprints, teeth, or leaf imprints on rocks. Paleontologists have been able to figure out what dinosaurs looked like by putting fossil bones together. It is like putting together a jigsaw puzzle.

Paleontologist Othniel Charles Marsh named *Stegosaurus* in 1877, after discovering its fossils in Morrison, Colorado. Paleontologists have learned a lot more about *Stegosaurus* since then. They have found two nearly complete *Stegosaurus* skeletons. They uncovered one in

Some of the earliest *Stegosaurus* fossils were found at this site in Morrison, Colorado.

Fremont County, Colorado, in 1886.

The second discovery, near Cañon City, Colorado, occurred in 1992. Paleontologists Bryan

Small and Ken Carpenter discovered a *Stegosaurus* skeleton missing only its front legs.

Part of a *Stegosaurus* skeleton displayed in the position in which it was found

It took seven weeks to remove the skeleton from the ground. The huge dinosaur was taken out in three sections. Workers removed the head and neck first and then the rest of the body. Miners, using drills as well as large pieces of equipment, helped remove the fossils from the ground.

In an interview with the author, Bryan Small said how excited he was about this find. "I liked dinosaurs when I was a kid and I just sort of got hooked." He enjoyed learning about dinosaurs so much that he became a paleontologist. After such a terrific discovery, it is easy to see how anyone could get hooked on dinosaurs.

# Extinction

Some people think that all dinosaurs became extinct, or died out, at the same time. But it didn't happen quite that way.

For about 180 million years, various kinds of dinosaurs existed. Yet no single kind of dinosaur lasted the entire time that dinosaurs were on Earth.

At the end of the Age of the Dinosaurs, all the remaining dinosaurs died out. It took about one million years for that to happen.

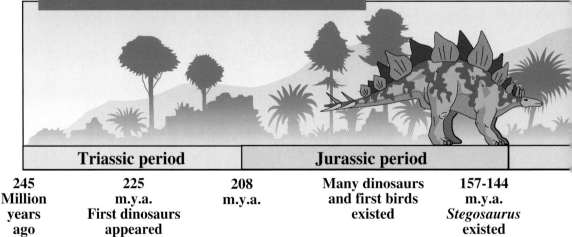

This timeline of prehistoric Earth shows when *Stegosaurus* lived.

| Triassic period | | Jurassic period | |
|---|---|---|---|
| 245 Million years ago | 225 m.y.a. First dinosaurs appeared | 208 m.y.a. | Many dinosaurs and first birds existed | 157-144 m.y.a. *Stegosaurus* existed |

There is no definite answer
to why the dinosaurs became
extinct. During the Age of the
Dinosaurs, Earth was still chang-
ing. The large landmasses called

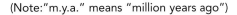

(Note:"m.y.a." means "million years ago")

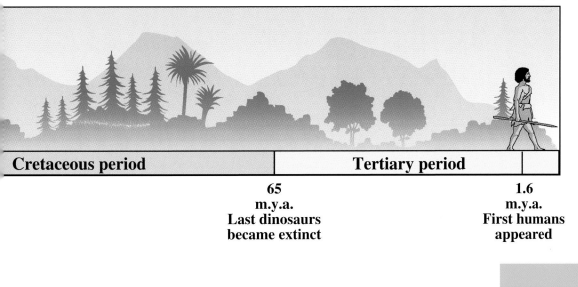

| Cretaceous period | Tertiary period | |
|---|---|---|

65
m.y.a.
Last dinosaurs
became extinct

1.6
m.y.a.
First humans
appeared

continents had not finished forming. Seas and mountain ranges were still taking shape. Different kinds of plant life appeared. The dinosaurs were likely unable to get used to all these changes.

Many paleontologists think that the dinosaurs became extinct after an asteroid crashed into Earth. Asteroids are large, rocky, planetlike bodies that move through space. If an asteroid struck

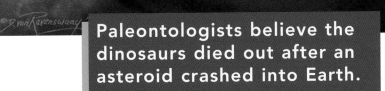

Paleontologists believe the dinosaurs died out after an asteroid crashed into Earth.

Earth, a huge crater, or hole, would have been created.

The dust from the crater would have floated up into the **atmosphere** to form thick, dark clouds. These clouds would have blocked out the sun. Earth would have become very cold. The dinosaurs probably could not have survived the cold temperatures.

*Stegosaurus* became extinct after being on Earth for more than 10 million years. People's interest in *Stegosaurus* has not

Museum displays of dinosaur skeletons attract many visitors.

died out, though. Today, museum exhibits, films, and books help us learn more about the armored dinosaur called *Stegosaurus*.

# To Find Out More

Here are some additional resources to help you learn more about *Stegosaurus*:

 **Books**

Benton, M. J. **Armored Giants**. Copper Beech Books, 2001.

Dalla Vecchia, Fabio Marco. **Stegosaurus**. Blackbirch Press, 2004.

Gray, Susan H. **Stegosaurus**. The Child's World, 2004.

Matthew, Rupert. **Dinosaurs Undercover**. Blackbirch Press, 2002.

O'Brien, Patrick. **Gigantic! How Big Were the Dinosaurs?** Henry Holt, 2002.

Schomp, Virginia. **Stegosaurus: And Other Plate-Backed Plant-Eaters.** Benchmark Books, 2004.

**Organizations and Online Sites**

### Fossils, Rocks, and Time
*http://www.geology.er.usgs. gov/eastern/fossils.html*

Visit this Web site to learn some fascinating fossil facts.

### Project Exploration
950 East 61st Street
Chicago, IL 60637
*http://www.info@project exploration.org*

This organization works to increase students' interest in paleontology.

### Stegosaurus—All About Dinosaurs
*http://www.pubs.usgs.gov/ gip/fossils/contents.html*

Check here for great information on *Stegosaurus*, fun quizzes, and some *Stegosaurus* craft projects.

# Important Words

*armored* equipped with a protective outer layer

*atmosphere* the blanket of gases that surrounds Earth

*fossils* evidence of plants and animals that lived long ago. Fossils might include bones, footprints, teeth, or leaf imprints on rocks.

*predators* animals that hunt other animals for food

*prehistoric* from the time before history was recorded

*prey* an animal that is hunted by another animal for food

*reptiles* cold-blooded animals that crawl on the ground or creep on short legs

# Index

# Meet the Author

Award-winning author Elaine Landau worked as a newspaper reporter, an editor, and a youth-services librarian before becoming a full-time writer. She has written more than 250 nonfiction books for young people, including True Books on animals, countries, and food. Ms. Landau has a bachelor's degree in English and journalism from New York University as well as a master's degree in library and information science. She lives with her husband and son in Miami, Florida.